POETRY

WWW.INDEPENDENTLEGIONS.COM

Jack is Back!

ISBN: 978-88-31959-73-5
OCTOBER 2020
COPYRIGHT (EDITION) ©2020 INDEPENDENT LEGIONS PUBLISHING
COPYRIGHT (WORK) ©2020 ALESSANDRO MANZETTI

EDITING: ANGELA YURIKO SMITH
COVER ART: WENDY SABER CORE
INTERIOR ILLUSTRATIONS: STEFANO CARDOSELLI

INCLUDING ALL NEW POEMS
EXCEPT FOR 'THE DARK KING'
PUBLISHED IN SPACE AND TIME MAGAZINE ISSUE 138 (2020)

POETRY

# I'M THE LAIR

I'm the Lair, I'm the dirty sidewalk

the overcrowded black star

of London's sky stuck to the ground.

Call me Whitechapel, sing my rhapsody

of shadows, rats and refugee.

Walk on me, go straight to the Ten Bells,

have a glass of something strong, warm

I'm the Lair, and this is my best Winter.


I'm the Lair, I'm the drum of reality

and like a prophet of misery,

living in a nest of dust, shillings and sweat,

I speak so many languages,

Which do you prefer, outsider?

English, Irish, Russian or maybe Jewish?

Walk on me, and keep your ears open.

I have a lot of stories for you.

I'm the Lair, I'm a weird reptile

with sixty-two red tails

[so many are the brothels here]

and twelve hundred tongues

to kiss an entire battalion at the same time

Call me Whitechapel, or Red Dragon

take off your shirt and show me your skin.

I'm the Lair, and this is my best Summer.


I'm the Lair, I'm the helper of the butcher

a pimp and a parish's altarboy.

Call me blood clot, pint of beer,

sawbones, gravedigger, brick wall

cockroach, brown bread or King of the Birds,

because you can see me everywhere.

I am anything that crawls, I am your guilty conscience

and this Autumn full of leaves and corpses.


I'm the Lair, the policeman with big mustache

and a robber who's about to getting drunk

counting money and victims on both hands.

I smell good, like a candy shop, but

on the other side of the sidewalk I may seem

so disgusting, in the form of a smallpox

on the face of a kid, which looks like the moon,

grey, blue, alien, filled with craters.

I'm a too old pregnant woman

beaten up by her husband, or you can see

my skinny figure behind the window of the asylum

where Spring never came.

# BLOODY RHAPSODY

Deep Red, Deep East End
smell of men and women
of misery, sweat and then the rainbow
of blood right after the knives's storms
and all shades of red, see,
violet, purple, amaranth and vermilion
splashed on the sidewalk
by the Titian of Whitechapel
who knows well all colors
flowing inside people
arteries, veins, ventricles, secret boxes
odalisques with white, warm skin
porcelain trained from life
in the universities of the alley
between cold kisses and whistles of policemen
wearing stiffened mustaches
with their heart always scared.

Deep Red, Deep East End
the ghost with the razor, Death

with a black and white face

and a necklace of sharp oyster shells

reading Shakespeare's sonnets

around every dark corner

blowing storms of hanging clothes

and the first five symphonies

of the spectre that everyone calls

The Ripper, tall and thin, short and fat

alive and dead, Jesus Christ and Lucifer

an angel with a blue tongue

or a demon with a long, coiled tail

lit like a fuse and ready to detonate

grenades of shouts, prayers

waking pimps in underwear and braces

who're sleeping under the sharp roofs

of London slowly dying, bled out.

# TALE OF A KIDNEY

London Hospital, October 16, 1888

*The kindley belonged to a female,*
concluded Dr. Openshow
after seeing the devil in a top hat
inside the lens of his microscope.
A devil? Here in Whitechapel?
It might explain that new red moon
days ago, a revolution of astrophysics.
*Do you remember, Old Boss?*
But he should be a magician, to color
a satellite that way, so remote place
in the black sky, with the same tint
of the sidewalk, while the pink eels of guts
covered it with blood, that night.

*The organ is human and having been*
*removed form the left side,*
wrote Dr. Openshow
after feeling a shiver down his spine.
The Devil is is often portrayed

as being left-handed, isn't that right?

He should love that side,

and he wanted to take away that part

with the right nature's position and mark.

*Big Boss*, the doctor whispered

talking to himself, *are you kidding me?*

Sometimes human minds need to see

wider skies, invisible and nonexistent gods,

and they ask for a touch of madness

to resist the north winds of days

or, in some cases, to survive

tides and drifts of organs and corpses

in the Acheron-colored wards of an hospital

with white hairs from fear.


*It had come from a woman about 45 years of age,*

*who also suffered from Bright's Disease,*

explained Dr. Openshow

while hearing a growl behind him.

Hey, is anyone there?

*No, you're wrong*, says the Old Boss,

another magician sewn into the consciousness

of the doctor, who's alone with his microscope

the kidney, and the shadows of midnight

able to build fake buildings, rides and bridges,

and all the terrible wonders of solitude.
Loneliness, an alley, a finger, a bone
of Withechapel's lair always lurking.
Loneliness, and then a half-naked soul smiling,
a black hat, a feather, a bright breast
caressed by lamp light.
A goddess with coal-smeared hands,
an imaginary wife, who must live
no longer than a second, like a sudden lightning.

*This disease is a failing of the kidneys*
*as a result of heavy drinking,*
said Dr. Openshow glancing
his bottle of whisky with the red label,
which looks like a motionless dancer
ready to stretch out its glass muscles
to follow a sudden rhapsody,
an exotic and sharp melody, the same
heard by the Ripper, with a mermaid
tattooed on his shoulder,
and a rosary of teeth in the left hand
which sound like little castanets.

# MAY SOME GENTLE MUSE WHISPER TO YOU LUCKY WORDS

*Close your eyes*

*and look homeward, Angel.*

Mr. Neardead paid four hundred pounds

to buy a virgin, a miracle, a rainbow for hire

[*I was just keeping her warm for you*,

said the brothel's keeper]

to refresh his memory of youth,

those days so shining, when you could feel

the grass between your toes,

when all things were synchronized

with the alien quartz of discovery.

*Touch my face,*

*and shatter my leaves before the new year.*

The little Angel, with eyes wide shut,

with its delicate fingers draws

an imaginary circle on Mr. Neardead's grey belly

[*Do whatever he wants*, said the brothel's keeper]

to create a magic well where to enter,

lowering down on a rope, to find his best years

now covered by a musty pavement

with the word LIFE written on it.


*May some gentle Muse*

*whisper to you lucky words.*

She, like a dart in the brain

shows to Mr. Neardead his old days

coated in dark, cold jelly

kept inside the past, hidden in the stomach

of the ghost of the young man he was.

[*Your first time, sweethart, it's worth ten times!*

whispered the brothel's keeper]

The little Angel turns into a mirror, enlarging its navel,

*Now look at you,* says to the client

smiling and revealing its milk teeth.


*The Muse herself,* so glassy,

enchants her octogenarian son

dancing, widening her purple petals

standing right in front of Mr Neardead.

[*This work... cu... cut out for you,*

stammers the brothel's keeper, spying the two].

She, like a thunder of morbid flesh,

lowers suddenly on him,

—a newborn carnivorous orchid—

legs open, screaming: *Give me all your syphilis!*

The little angel turns into a white tiger,

stretching its fingernails.

*Now look at me*, it roars to Mr. Neardead

while sticking its fingers in his old, frightened eyes,

down to the roots, pulling the optic nerves

as if they were the reins of its destiny.

[*Holy shit!* shouts the brothel's keeper,

with dropped trousers.]

Blind, dark sorrow, repainted with the ghostly orange

of a freshly peeled apricot, and…

little hands (those of an Angel), dripping

with polluted blood

and stained with coal and whale oil,

finally motionless.


*Look to the future Angel,*

*your sorrow is not dead today.*

# THE BUTCHER'S SHOP

Mrs. Askmore comes inside my shop

every day, at any time

with her old-fashioned green hat,

inside which are hidden little monsters,

translucent rubbery worms

with large ears and antennas

(they record every sound)

and a brain the weight of a gram.

Mrs. Askmore loves gossip,

and takes away bunches of the words

in the big pockets of her black coat

(she's a gravedigger for rumors)

She has a dead kiss on her lips,

and loves to see poorer women than her.


Mrs. Lovelone is a witch,

she buried four husbands, really,

and some say that one day she cooked

the heart of the first of them

for some kind of spell for immortality.

But... I guess that didn't work out,

given that she's getting older and older
and the other three husbands
are playing cards in the same coffin
of West Norwood Cemetery block 47
with their shortened legs.
Mrs Lonelone often asks for liver sausages
and smells like ointment and talcum powder.

Mrs. Whalebread is my favorite,
she's rich and fancy but, above all
so fat, so much flesh driven
by only one spirit; she's a miracle,
the Ark of Covenant, for a butcher like me.
Tuesday is her day here, late morning
always accompanied by a man named Erazm,
a Russian servant with blackened teeth
and greedy, suspicious eyes.
Mrs. Whalebread never looked me
straight in the eye, I'm less than nothing for her,
not even the fresher piece of meat of my shop.

And then there's me, the butcher
the master of knives and bones
with my white apron, see me,
stained with blood, signed by the innards

of tasty animals and lonely women,

ladies with wide hips, the smiling of Magdalene

on their faces, that skin of burnt amber

which hides iron hearts and soft membranes.

Unknown Pulsar and fat pleasures.

But I have the keys, the blades, the clamps

for all those creatures, for each polluted rose.

I know well where beauty like to hide itself:

between the scarlet curtains of a belly

full of pulsating treasures.

Olympia, Salome, listen to me,

It's almost night.

# MAGDALENE, OLYMPIA, SALOME

Magdalene, Olympia, Salome,
listen to me, it's almost night.

The hooves of a horse, an open window
an opera song from Verdi's Tosca,
the leather rage of a drunk husband
and then, fifty yards ahead,
the silence of a contaminated alley
under a hallway of sky without stars.

There, around the corner,
between Whitechapel's thighs,
the syphilis demon, hidden in the body
of a red-eyed rat,
climbs on human shoulders
to whisper forbidden dreams,
while the wheels of a chariot accelerate.

The night is molten metal
ready to be forged, sharpened.
A door that closes, a baby cry.

A policeman, who looks like a blue ghost,

coughs making his helmet wobble

and the Queen Victoria Jubilee Medal of 1887

hanging on the left shoulder of his uniform.


She, Miss Four Penny,

curly red hair, eyes big like Byzantine coins,

the kind of 'fallen woman' loved by Charles Dickens,

interviewed by him, and maybe groped in secret,

she's impatient, wringing her fingers

bitting her lips, with a crucifix god under her blouse.


The night has diamonds in its mouth

and a long black tail; now she's alone

hears my footsteps, looks back to me

and smiles, my Mona Lisa with broken teeth.

She was just beaten by her master, you see,

or maybe by her husband, for a too bland soup.


Too skinny, and too beautiful...

My razor doesn't hurt such portraits,

when nature has done its job well

and only the devil has spoiled everything.

No, she doesn't fit as one of my still lifes

made of pieces of pavement, human organs,

and intestines like silk scarves,
my beloved trained, shining pythons.

Messalina, Lady Hamilton, Salome,
listen to me, I'm the Ripper.

# The God with the Black Hat

None but other lonely hearts
can know my sadness, the cold
I felt that night, when I was born,
when the blade cut my soft armor,
the pericardium, showing me the outside
world, making me come to light.

I rembember his red hands,
the bed floating in a sea of blood,
its shallow water, and smooth
white linen rocks, over and under
the corpse of a big creature, bitten
by a school of carnivorous fish,
or something like that.

The god with the black hat, my father
took me away from that red chaos
showing me Whitechapel alleys
the night, the ancient stars up there,
and finally hidden me in his pocket

which smelled of dark freedom, beer,

pickled pollack and Irish tobacco.


I didn't think the outside world

was so beautiful, magical,

but I saw it for a few seconds,

so you can undertand me when I say

than only lonely hearts, which have seen

the stars disappear, or fell in love with ghosts,

can know my sadness,

now that I'm trapped in this glass globe,

forced to drink trasparent alcohol,

and to imagine me like a virgin.

under the gaze of my horrible god.


*In memory of Marie Jeanette Kelly*

# Sick Rhapsody

Deep Red, Deep East End
inside hospitals and corridors
where Syphilis runs with her sisters
all shouting like crazy, piercing
pillows, membranes and fingers
without wedding rings
while giant leeches, fat with blood
are sleeping under the signs of pharmacies
and places where miracles happen
where the Virgin Lady appears so beautiful
and simple, stained with human coal
with calluses on her hands
wearing a long gown dotted
with stars, stones and shillings
on a blue background edged with gold
that doesn't look like the sky up there.

Deep Red, Deep East End
in the houses where old people
and children scream and die
old people and children, knotted by magic

in the same thread of life

while the scissors approaching

with the black hands of tuberorcolosis

cold as Winter, the general

perpetually at war with its saber

made of frost, snow, fever

hissing in the air to cut into slices

green ghosts of hope, invisible hearts

close to the stoves, in a poor home

trying to survive the night

swallowing the liquor of melancholy

which tastes like nettle, honey, poppy

and trains leaving.

# MARY ANN

August 31, 1888

She was five foot seven, tall, with brown hair
and gray thoughts, here and there,
dark eyes, and reddish cheeks
friends of cheap wine and pimp slaps.
Her teeth were missing, but not so
her biting words, which cursed someone up there,
maybe the Lord of Destiny.

That warm corpse was Mary, called Polly
dressed with a black straw bonnet
trimmed with black velvet and sad smiles,
a brick-red overcoat, which looked like
the guesthouse sign on Flower and Dean Street,
(stay the hell away from that place!),
ribbed black wool tights, a flannel petticoat
and men's boots with iron toes.

The sidewalk lying at number 51 of Buck's Row
has the memory of an elephant, it had seen Polly
cursing angels and demons, and then
try to scratch a face of shadow,
a stranger with sharp steel fingers.
Maybe it was that Lord of Destiny
tired of hearing her bad words,
determined to cut that sticky, dirty connection
with Whitechapel's lair.
There are more beautiful places in the world
when you're a god, and you can choose.

That corpse, now with his arms
warm from the elbows up,
and the face facing east,
she was a tragic woman, a kind of
Madame Bufferfly who has never seen a ship
a charming captain, not even the sea itself,
but the blizzard inside her child heart
had given birth to too different dreams
compared to Whithechapel's crooked tracks
which always lead to the same alley.
No red kimono, no flowers, no opera in those places.

The god of that night was a long-bladed knife

accurate like a Mozart composition.

It had taken Polly's neck, ten inches of sharp running,

and then it had drawn a meat well

under the left ear of the woman,

to show the vertebrae to the stars,

those collapsed roots of everyday.

That corpse was Mary, with her dead hands

gripped to an iron gate she had failed to cross,

but it was a trick, a show for the police;

Polly, wrapped in a black wedding dress,

with the snaking eyes of Medusa,

she had really crossed the threshold, in seconds

and had disapperead, like the illusion of something

running along the blurred horizon.

# ANNIE

September 8, 1888


An alley that crosses two buildings,

a bloody courtyard, a five-foot high palisade

some coins on the ground, an abandoned leather apron,

and then, in the middle, Annie's corpse,

like the sculpture of a red and violet still life,

with an handkerchief around her neck,

what she had waved, a few seconds earlier,

from the imaginary balcony of a black ship,

to greet the planet earth in a hurry.

She had beautiful teeth.


A man who crosses an alley, running,

powered by a wind which smells of strawberry tree honey.

A knife in his hand, with a long and thin blade,

and a coat, full of treasures of pleasures, soft and warm,

which seems winged, able to making him disappear

as fast as a shot, leaving there

the last traces of his cascading thoughts:

"She had beautiful teeth"


*Annie, can you hear me?*

Asks her Fortune 199, her drunk guardian angel

rushed to the spot with its curled up wings

and the crazy, errant, confused gaze of a tramp.

She can't hear, no more,

[try another way, poor angel, with your golden melody]

she can't stop staring with dead blue eyes

at those four lighted windows

which hide figures of sacred people.

*She had beautiful teeth,* thinks the angel.


Annie, a too modern sculpture

for both the living and the dead,

something never seen before

by Phoenician or Victorian eyes, a motionless dancer

with legs drawn up, and feet resting on the ground.

No one can see her music, her beauty,

she got sucked up by a vortex

and shot up into the sky, like an iron bird,

toward a new constellation, where

her slashed throat and the mutilated Venus' equipments

are not so alien, where good satellites

they start spinning around her beautiful teeth,

like flies in love.

Look up there, those distant ivory lights.


[29, Hanbury Street]

# Dear Boss

September 25, 1888

Dear Boss,
I keep on hearing the police
have caught me, but
they are dead wrong,
I'm in my lair, always thirsty
under a strong roof and
the wing of a wild fortune,
on the other side of the city,
a good secret place
away from their shiny boots
following wrong tracks.

No prison bars here,
only huge pagodas, containing
greenhouses of thoughts and desires,
full of red and violet fruits,
instead of damp cells.
So much space, in my home

and inside my head,

so many doors and windows wide open

showing me rooftops, lusty sunsets

speechless angels hanging with ropes

on streets corners, like living torches.


That joke about leather apron

gave me real fits, but

if you really want to defy me

I know many little games, ah ha,

that will make you laugh so much

to unpick the smile from your face,

shaking your bowels to the point

of making you vomit your heart.


I am down on whores, a lone wolf,

and I shant quit ripping them

'till I finish my still life galleries

turning the alleys to museums,

allowing many eyes, even the poorest,

to admire the show without a ticket.

I am a firework,

and you're the damn sad water

that ruins all the fun.

I saved some of the red stuff

of a strangled Muse, my last job,

in a ginger beer bottle, to write you with,

but it went thick like glue ...

and so I used that inspired pulp

to form a little ocean of innocence,

(you dont' know my place, and my bathtub)

to dive into, between the amaranth waves

of killed memories and bubbles of cries,

of breaths, dreams and castrated moments.

So, red ink is fit enough I hope,

what you think, Boss?


The next job I do

I shall clip the ladys ears off

and send to the police officers.

Or, maybe they prefer something else...

the left ventricle? Heart is more dramatic,

perhaps wrapping it in a sheet of newspaper

mixing ink, words, blood,

emotions, fear and oxygen's ghosts.

It would be a big hit if,

opening my wet pack,

Scotland Yard could hear

that piece of heart talk, saying that

there is too much noise around,

and that the Whitechapel Red Circus,

itinerant like a young Jesus,

is arrived, to put everyone back seated

on their own uncertain fate,

getting them wondering

what Hell really is,

and from what kind of womb,

(and the exact color and race of it)

we all came out to see this world,

and then to die.


Good Luck.


Yours truly
Jack the Ripper

# TEN BELLS

Reclaim your night, try that place

the 'Jack the Ripper' pub,

before it changes its name again,

[*Ten Bells*, but were eight after the fire]

or it may disappear, devoured

by the Christ Church next door

with its holy teeth as long as organ pipes.

Reclaim the night, look over there

in front of the entrance you'll find Annie

fishing for clients, off-duty priests and murderers,

aimless ghosts with no more stars to look at,

mesmerized by her beautiful teeth.

Reclaim your night, enter and sit down

near Mary Jane, the life of the party

who dresses a weird suit made of night moths,

with a rope around her large waist

from which ten keys hang.

Pick one of them, and you'll see what happens.

Mister Holmes, a fur trader with a reddish scalp,

with a deep love line on his left hand,

has chosen the key number six;

Now he's looking, full of hope and beer,

at the yellow ceiling of a poor pension

waiting for one of Gauguin's little goddesses.

*'I assure you, my sister is eleven!*

*She has gold teeth, none are missing.'*

Mary Jane's trick number six.


Reclaim your night, get some drinks

to the shy specter of June,

the girl dead in the Thames, inside a sack,

[a virgin is worth many shillings,

and if you pay you can do what you want]

who camouflages herself like a crucifixion of leaves,

between the blue and white floral patterns

of the decorated wall of the north side.

You will recognize her by the smell, so intense

of basil, mint, and you will see her coal eyes

blink open at midnight

[they will no longer be simple corollas, dead paints]

on that beautiful Victorian mural of painted tiles,

to observe the clients, looking among them

the culprit of her murderous river current,

of that burlap spineless coffin.

If you see June, please whisper in her ear

that I'm always thinking about our first time;

it was like a liquid dream, a red sunflower

blossomed from my satisfied belly.


[33, Church Street]

# ELIZABETH

September 30, 1888


Long Liz, my Swedish wind

pale, curly Lutheran she-devil

here we are not in your gaunt Gothenburg

65 krona brought you here,

riding on tides and currents,

and 65 stab wounds I promised you, do you remember?

No, you can't, I just thought it,

that afternoon in Mr. HackFate's shop

your hands so long, white

caressing the fabrics, sensually...

I was behind you, sucking with my nostrils

your mantis perfume.


Long Liz, my Swedish wind

ran away too fast

blown by a merciful and perverse god

who doesn't know the pleasure of pain

and underestimates the money of destiny.

What happened to your suitor,

the alcoholic cop who hits harder

than a professional boxer?

The ghost of your husband, the tuberculous,

escaped from the cellars

of the Poplar and Stepney Sick Asylum,

did he slit the throat of the bastard? Or the tongue?

And what happened to you, away from my eyes

just when the fun was starting.


Long Liz, my Swedish wind

my stuttering tiger

with six pence in the pocket

and your black crepe bonnet,

black like the fine jacket,

that I splashed with red roses.

*'No. Not tonight. Some other night'*

you said to that guy in the long coat

a grey wolf in human clothing,

it was because you were waiting for me, just me ...

No, you couldn't know, it was in my mind

like your blood, sealed in there,

so clear and fluid, that Sunday,

the same color and density, brilliance,

that slipped out of the tap in your neck.

You would say anything but your prayers.


[Berner Street]

# Entangled Rhapsody

Deep Red, Deep East End

nine hundred thousand entangled souls

in a large infected clod

of the planet earth, with the navel

formed in Miter square, and legs and arms

stretched like sidewalks and twisted alleys

trampled by men with big hands

who earn a pound a week

where women are on sale, a piece

at a time, quick ten-shilling marriages

imprisoned by the rows of Huguenot houses

with a brick belly and head

and a pointed black hat on their heads

covered with slate and burnished climbing plants

while the rumors of Spitalfields Market

the polluted brain of the East End

with its wooden stalls of meats

poultry, roots, and behind them

sergeants of the now-now with their ankles

chained by the day after tomorrow, and five children

to feed who throw dreams and stones

with their slingshots, from Dorset Street

up to the spine of Fournier Street

with its synagogue in the shape of a Masonic temple

painted with prayers the only building there

without a gin store where they sell

stories as old as time

embroidered on fabrics, hung like brooches

on skinny mothers in work-houses

with their shriveled breasts sucked by strangers

and third degree relatives, locked up between

walls stuffed with opium jelly of memories

and fresh rosemary still sprouting

despite everything, in the fields behind Brick Lane

from where you can see green heads and thoughts

behind the windows of the old insane asylum

entangled among blackberry bushes.

# No Wedding Ring

September 32, 1888

The surgeon, with clear blood on his hands

made after the young girl giving birth

[a blossoming of a steel corolla,

a forceps without petals]

licks his fingers whispering heretic:

'Mmmmm, blood doesn't die so soon

like the brain, and that's a good thing'.

A silent room, a home of despair

a solitary wooden crucifix, flies,

two sacks of potatoes, a skinny dog sleeping,

dreaming of new bones, human or not.

The surgeon turns towards

the unfortunate young mother

[she dead when her baby, slippering,

was still on its way to see the outside world]

and smiles, because she looks like a stockfish

with that pale face, the grey skin,

and all muscles and flesh in plaster.

[the Black Lady had made her as rigid as stone,

using special balsams, and magic glue]

Then, the surgeon bends down

to unscrew the cap of a green bottle

resting on a chair: Absinthe? Cheap wine?

His throat is dry, and feels some little paws

moving inside his infested neck.

It's a cockroach, small like an atom,

which is climbing the carotid

to reach his big mouth;

It's a microscopic messenger,

wearing a shining amethyst's armor,

sent there by the demon which lives inside the man

hidden in the furnace of his guts,

like a coiled snake.

*Hey, I'm here! Do not ignore me!*

Then other noises, and a voice.

'Doctor, there is another girl to examin'.

says his assistant, Mrs. Hardpeat

just returned to the room, after having drained

in secret, another green bottle,

hidden in the bathroom, behind a holy icon

which depicts the Virgin Mary,

fortunately with her eyes closed.


'Another one? Pregnant? Okay, okay, let's go see.'

grumbles the surgeon walking down the hall

the gut number seven of that 'workhouse'.

A desert full of doors and rooms, no hope.

'Mmmmm, she is a good-looking girl;

[the heretic has turned on his possessed view]

Where did she come from?' he asks

while his demon is swelling its coils

and all the purple diamonds on its skin.


'She was brought here last night,'

replies the old woman, coughing up seconds,

"she was found lying in the street. Where she come from,

or where she was going to, nobody knows.'

The surgeon leans over the body, like a reptile

and raises the left hand. She looks like a holy figure.

[strange noises now, maybe rattles?]

"The old story," he says, shaking his head:

"No wedding ring, I see.'

'Please leave me alone with her, Madame'.

[silence, and then the gong of lust].

While the old woman leaves the room

with little steps, like a pigeon

scampering among the crumbs,

the demon inside the man stretches its coils,

knowing that soon it will be able to jump out

from that anthropomorphic shell,

and to get drunk on reality [Wow]

swilling buckets of bourbon, of young lives.

Another silent room, a circus of despair

a solitary window showing the last night,

an old copy of Dicken's Oliver Twist,

[the first chapter missing, ripped off]

two jars of chickpea, a perverse surgeon,

worse than the demon which possessed him,

who's enjoying, naked, the corpse of a still fresh Venus

—her legs apart, and a blackened diamond

hidden deep inside her womb—

cold like snow, warm like Hell,

so delicious like poverty, sometimes.


[When the street have no name]

*Thanks to Charles Dickens, and his 'Oliver Twist,' for having inspired some lines.*

# CATHERINE



September 30, 1888


Dark auburn hair, hazel eyes,

you're pretty, drunk Joan of Arc.

You have chosen to go left

in the direction of Aldgate, not home;

you smelled me, the ultimate temple

full of forbidden spices and ingots of flesh,

and I felt your skin slipping

at every step, upon your pounded bones

by those police scoundrels.

I like your blue tattoo, Catherine,

I wish your lips were blue too...

Let me open your belly, to discover

the color of your liver, of kidneys

and of your shipwrecked heart.

Are they all blue too? If so, who painted them?

I want to color you inside, changing you

and to take away with me a portrait,

a still warm pulsing, a memento

of human grams cut still alive,

like raspberries and blackberries of forbidden Eden,

pieces of who you are, of who you were,

and what you will become

carved by my iron brushes.

Oh, let me dream, make me a Da Vinci

and don't tighten your muscles, while

I will make art of you, from throat to groin.


[near Miter Square]

# Saucy Jacky Postcard

October 15, 1888


I was not codding dear old Boss

when I gave you the tip...

you'll hear tomorrow about

my double flight:

two Magdalenes lost their voice,

throat and kisses to sell.

I didn't have time

to explore the first one, the Swedish

with low and clear skies in her eyes

those of the North, even if she was so warm.

But don't worry,

with the other it went better,

I explored her, with the periscope of folly,

I looked inside her

and saw all her purple and red molecules

bubbling with life, and then run away

leaping on dirty sheets,

and so, like frightened, sticky liquid,

spilling on the floor of that room,

the Antinferno with only one window

overlooking the everyday life,

with a floor trodden by too much feet

like the one of Sistine Chapel.

There is also a relic now, there

listen up, Boss... don't forget;

under the boards, well hidden,

her heart lies, buried dry and cold,

frightening even the ghosts

with its beating, without any logic;

That Magdalene must have read Poe,

or watched through the narrow peephole

of immortality.

Weird secrets strangled too soon.


Thanks for keeping last letter back

till I got to work again.


Jack the Ripper

# FROM HELL

October 15, 1888


*Mr Lusk,*

*Sor, I send you half the Kidne*

*I took from one women*

*prasarved it for you.*

Look at it, hold it in your hand, without gloves

bring it close to your ear, like a shell

and you can feel the sea of Hell,

not just a lake, or a curve of Acheron,

where in boiling waters

memories and old terrestrial stories are fried.

Do you hear them crackle?

It's a new sound, right?

No, they don't feel pain anymore,

but anyway they can't scream,

and open their tongueless mouths

yawning smoke, before melting.

This is how all things end,

but the hunt for the monster is always open.

*Tother piece of the Kidne I fried and ate,*

*it was very nise*, and much smaller

once cooked, it was lonely in the huge pan,

like me, raw meat waiting for

the flame, the tropic of cancer,

the skilled fingers of a Russian cook,

a foreigner, like everyone else here,

putting me on the grill

among the embers, in a cauldron of my size.

*I may send you the bloody knif*

*that took out the Kidne,*

but it's the leader, and gives orders.

I call it Brother of Steel

because the other, the man in flesh and blood,

was ridden by violet goddess syphilis

and now is locked in a padded room

alone, in his soft pan,

along with potatoes, onions, a

notebook to drawing monsters

and a old family photo;

I'm the tallest one, with a straight face,

gritting my teeth, waiting for

my mother's boiling water tricks,

a hundred degrees purification

(Pray to Jesus and Madgalene!)

twice a week, in the home cellar

between funnels and strange holy water soups,

with her familiar breath on my young face
while she rotates back her eyes, like a shark.

*Catch me when you can Mishter Lusk*

# MARY JANE
### [A VIOLET FROM MOTHER'S GRAVE]

63

November 9, 1888

Ginger, don't move please

not even a muscle,

don't breathe, the beauty could escape from you

it's so easy to ruin everything.

You still smell of the Land of France

and your hair is getting redder

each passing second.

New blood and innate nature,

what a marvel of living and dead cells

of membranes and organs in turmoil.

Only torment? No, you know

this is a liberation, a free flight

over the roofs and filth of this coal-toothed

district, which dreams with pincers,

razors and shillings under the pillow.

Now I have carved you in my mind

like a Rembrandt's portrait;

you will be beautiful forever, as good as new,

with that opalescent complexion

[you're my Orient Express, my Constantinople]

and the puffs of freckles on your nose.

Now sing that song again

*'A Violet from Mother's Grave'*

let me hear your strangled voice

that of a fresh specter, so subtle...

it doesn't matter, my imagination is a giant

and can feel the vibrating legs of a grasshopper

ready to jump on a leaf of a remote island,

a place hidden among the haunted Tropics

of my glue, of my mist, of my desert

that undress everything, in seconds.

Tahiti, Paris, Jerusalem,

if only there was a safe place where,

making drunk the ogre who holds me in chains,

I'll be able to walk by myself, holding my breath

long enough to reach the white or black shore,

towards which, Ginger, you're soaring,

bloody, like all the others.


[Miller's Court, 13]

# MADHOUSE RHAPSODY

Deep Red, deep East End

stories of asylums, green ghosts

and white brains attached

to the lean bodies where they are sealed

to the trees in the courtyard

wearing hard straitjackets

with leather sleeves

and a number printed on the chest

waiting for the hour of bloodletting

and the cautery at the nape with caustic potash

smeared between the thighs of women

without menstruation without hair

who dream wet dreams

sleeping into wooden crates with straw

or into cages for hysterics and fools

in which a strange rhapsody resonates

a melody of inertia and lunar landscapes

of old stories and distant love songs

of America and Mexico and Paris

while the children of syphilis

with their alien ocelot skin

forged by alien methane's lakes and

rancid blood of frontline soldiers

and the troops of epileptics with

an ice bag tied on their heads

which makes them think about North

towards which the asylum always faces

with the funeral ropes

of the first symphony of the young Mahler

a place always open to the public

who pays the ticket to enter

with shiny shoes and a demiurge's erection

to the carnival of madmen and rebels

to enjoy the show and all the symphonies

of bromide and incontinence

and splinters of reality under the skin

extracted with pliers by doctors with clean hands

with a tiny dry sunflower in their pocket

that a while ago looked South.

# The Angel in Buck's Row

August 31, 1888


*Don't do it*, says the blue-eyed boy

from the rooftop playground of the Board Shool.

Afternoon, Jack sniffs the gray air

of Buck's Row, observing his shadow

on the line of cottages on the left,

inhabitated by ghosts still alive.

Here, he thinks, here you can smell the honey

of what is fading, fading away.

Honey, chestnuts and dark bread.

The life which tries to shorten the legs of Death.


*Don't do it, it's a pity*, says the blue-eyed boy

over there, behind the rusty railing.

Jack looks up, hears that subtle voice

haunting him for hours, a curse

with a mouth full of baby teeth;

such a stupid divine spell.

Here, he must be here, he thinks,

tonight, when Buck's Row will transform itself

in a forge of cheap lovers and diamonds,

making the street swallow man's juice.


*Don't do it, she will scream!* says the blue-eyed boy

up there, rising from the building

with his wings made of newsprint.

Jack lowers his eyes, that angel

shines too much, blinding his special vision:

she, Magdalene, Salome, Olympia,

on the sidewalk, with the throat cut,

and the night dancing around her

dressed in a skeleton suit,

with the North Star gripped between its teeth.


[Buck's Row, everywere]

# She Knew my Name

*Freely inspired by 'The Raven' by Edgar Allan Poe*

On a dark night, while I pondered, excited

on unusual ancient volumes of anatomy,

sometimes raising my eyes to my beloved

illustrations of human slaughter

by De Bry Brothers, hanging in front of me

on the noblest wall of this studio,

—a symposium of proteins, blood and butterflies of souls—

suddenly I heard a knock on my door.

A nocturne, unexpected visitor,

was besieging my sacred lair.

How had he found me?

"Jack!" said a woman's voice, back there,

cold like that frozen December.


She knew my name —but nothing more

because in my exquisite London I wander like a shadow

in the humid maze of my neighborhood,

and I don't have any friends other than alleys,

the Thames and its rats without human thoughts,

the windows illuminated by the lamps revealing

the insides of the lives of others, of those who live

lives that I can't tolerate, as if they were

dissonant and arrogant peppercorns, scattered

on a perfect plate —the balance of solitude, my North Star.


"Jack!" repeated the woman's voice, not giving up.

So, I grabbed my razor opening the shutters, to see

stretching the neck and a tentacle of soul,

if there really was a visitor out there, or if in my head

the Maenads, my blooded guardian angels —thoughts made by cognac]

they were just partying with their subtle voices,

who know how to break borders,

moving from brain to brain

I leaned out, but saw only the wind —nothing more

and the blade of my razor, which tells present and future.

That time it wouldn't suggest nothing —the blade was bare, and didn't shine.]


But then, magically, a severed head came out of nowhere,

flying — it had to be so — thanks to the engines of my imagination.]

Not even looking at me, that miffed Medusa,

without the least semblance of ceremony, she rushed into my room]

hovering in mid-air, and then changed her course

heading towards the bust of Pallas above the door.

She took the place of its marble face, and from her livid mouth

purple, watered down by death, I heard the word: "Nevermore."


Oh, taking a closer look at the distorted features of that face

without a body, which must had gone through at least three
doors:]

the Hell's one, so boiling, that of Death, cold and sharp,

and before these, the one of street life, with its bas-reliefs

of thousand hands tearing soft pink flesh, I had a wince.

I wasn't wrong: inside the eyes of my mysterious Medusa,

were (still) imprinted a top hat, a black cloak, and scalpel

which like an angel's ray descended from above to below.

—two vivid pictures, the last things she saw in her life—

"Elizabeth, is that you?" The most beloved of the loved!

the purest and warmest bowels,

a sanctuary of flesh, that took me back.

And such melancholy arises, surrounded again by

an old siege that make resonate the castanets of pleasure,

throwing incendiary darts, beyond the walls,

of renewed obsessions.


"Elizabeth, is that you?" But my beloved, who came from

the shores of the Night, said 'Nevermore'

without moving her lips, speaking to my mind.

Therefore I approached that Medusa, of who my memory

still exhumed the scent of salty apricot of ther intimate door,

and the towers of her open belly, which jealously held tight

the bowels, on which fell snowflakes and insane drops of myself.

"Talk to me" I begged her, "What do you want on these
terrestrial shores?"]

But my beloved, that phantom head, vanished as it came,

but she had not visited me in vain.

Every morning, in front of the mirror, I look in love

the mark of her invisible bite, right here, on the neck.

It mights seems a pledge of love, if they hat not been

marks of Plague's teeth.

# The Son of Cordial Godfrey

You touched me, Purple Goddess
here, above the navel,
your flower of flesh has sprung up
like a splendid ulcer, a memento
of that ghostly opium den
in which a Salome, who called herself Lucy.
had danced for everyone.

Now you are inside me, every day
and I might love you as well,
purple hotbed of pain and passion,
shiny wound, pustule of morbid memories.
But, you see, my heart can't have an owner,
it is the slave of an invisible tyrant
which never misses something:
Opium, the Achilles' shell of times like these.

So, I have to kill you, Goddess Syphilis
before you kill me.
I won't use stupid Dover's Powder,

or others dust spell.
I am a gentleman, I have read Sir Bacon
and Shakespeare; maybe that's why
tragedy fascinates me more than ordinary happiness.

The little boy, my twelve-year-old medicine,
bought with the same price of a good horse,
is waiting for me naked in bed, stunned
by a drop of the old Cordial Godfrey.
After him, you will disappear too
in the same short coffin, with his poor carcass
dry, no longer miraculous.
They will say it was a bad cold.
in Whitechapel people die from these things.

But here and now, in front of this mirror
where I'm looking at you,
admiring your heretic beauty,
surrealist portrait on my so trivial skin,
so bourgeois, like a family Sunday,
I swear I'll never forget
your hot lips, and your infected messenger
Salome, Lucy with her golden eyes,
shapely and unnatural vapor,
born between coils of opium.

# ALICE
### [LITTLE IS KNOW OF YOU]


July 17, 1889


Little is known of you, Alice

but I counted all your freckles

one by one, for whole days.

Nobody pays much attention to me,

I'm so ordinary, thin as air,

and I always go unnoticed

like the death of a stranger.


Little is known of you, Alice

but they should remember

that July night in London

when we couldn't breathe from the heat

and inside the Whitechapel nest

three eggs hatched, one after the other.

Poison, the blood of misery.


Little is known of you, Alice

and of the snakes born that night,

young, inexperienced reptiles

with a great desire to live and bite.

One of them crawled up to you

attracted to your French perfume.

You were dressed like Olympia.


Little is known of you, Alice

and many think it was me

to take your life away, together with

a piece of your Mount of Venus.

But nobody blinks twice at me,

evanescent like a summer dream,

not even a snake on its first hunt.


Little is known of you, Alice

of the many days I spent following you

and all the nights waiting,

motionless like a quadrant of sky

when you offerered yourself to all,

jumping on the first boat coming along...

That captain, looking for any star,

had never seen you before.


Little is known of you, Alice

and of that snake number two

yellowish, already sick for some time,

left-handed like the devil,

which cut your left carotid artery

as an amateur, like a lover who

after having spent ten years in jail

stands finally in front of his aged Diva.

Too much haste, and too little depth.


Little is known of you, Alice

but I saw you dying

and your left breast blooming blood,

but no one notices me, you see

I'm a frameless mirror

into which that serpent had looked

to see his name written in the newspaper,

to kill another useless day ready to start.

Friend snakes, killers and rippers, crawl

and bring my name to history,

like the Mona Lisa.


[Castle Alley]

# WHITECHAPEL RHAPSODY

Deep Red, deep East End

overcrowded houses strangled

by hanging clothes, ropes and beads

green painted insane asylums,

hordes of toothless poor people

riding horses, locomotives and whores

fast as razors and slow as cancer

in the faded alleys of Whitechapel

under the chimneys, the reddish roofs

among the rows of rusty graves of people

still alive, where it comes from

scent of chestnuts, and a big man

with the white hat of a cheesecutter

who's the king of those four ways

a cross of passages, of upside down shops

a sign that shines like a diamond

the opium den, next to a pub

showing a denture made of black pots

and red flowers, with its shop windows

capturing passersby, equine and human eyes

hearses, skinny bicycles.

Deep Red, deep East End

the factories, the anguished gates

lips smeared with charcoal

a potato soup and a wife to beat up

who sells postcards and their own breasts

on the shore of the morning when

prayers in Russian are spilled on the street

together with buckets of blood and soap

jump between pools, steal a donut

the whistle of a policeman, the whisper

of a whore wearing a hussar hat

and the cries of hospital's wards and floorboards,

where Madame Syphilis walks on tiptoe

fucking you at night, with her magic hammer

the relief, the night shift and the out of hours brain

of a madman at the window at dawn

who counts his fingers and the eyes already awake

who meet by chance, to live or die.

# THE DARK KING

I am the Dark King,

the mud that takes a thousand forms

which can become, at will

with an injection of Apollinare's adrenaline,

a three-eyed fetish man,

a flying calf with golden hooves,

a well-endowed Wagner, an apocalyptic Viking

with a long beard stained with wind,

or the boiling teeth of a chainsaw

drunk with gasoline and marrow juice

dressing a steel miniskirt.

[I talk, I growl, I lick and shear]

I am the Dark King

who whispers obscenity in many ears,

and requiem, blues, jazz (or a forbidden Tosca)

of hot and cold bodies surprised

by a deluge of psychedelic Montrachet

and knives stuck and twisted

inside fake boobs, black and white hearts

missing in art galleries and sewers.

I am a laughing Lacrimosa

with my transgender Mozart, but I'm

at the same time, the bald, short-tailed dog

which follows your idiot funeral.

[I sing, I cut, I kill and bark]


I am the Dark King

a drunken Ingres who paints odalisques

with green nipples and phosphorescent clitoris

(I have new colors, and Saturn's figs);

I'm the one who bites slumbered buttocks

making them to bleed from kykeon,

wet dreams, goddesses' cellulite paté.

I am the dwarf of a circus,

with monkey hands and platinum brain,

or the last cyclops inside the Sistine Chapel

pledged to pluck and boning angels,

with rosary beads and chicken feathers

between my teeth.

[I spit bones and tasteless brains, I paint and smear]


I am the Dark King

who wrote stories on the fallopian tubes of the Bastille,

on cathedrals of flesh and

subway benches painted with blasphemies.

I am the oyster, the rod, the fingers of a pimp,

a guardian devil with a big mouth

and the Bukowski's drunk stomach.

Don't worry, take between your teeth

this ticket to a grotesque Musée D'Orsay

full of iridescent French and Tahitian vulvas.

I am Olympia, a naked lunch, an AK47

that shoots on what you hide.

I am your dark side.

## ABOUT THE AUTHOR

ALESSANDRO MANZETTI, (Rome, Italy) is a Two-time Bram Stoker Award-winning author, editor, and translator of horror fiction and dark poetry whose work has been published extensively in Italian and English, including novels, short and long fiction, poetry, essays, graphic novels and collections.

English publications include his novels *Shanti - The Sadist Heaven* (2019) and *Naraka - The Ultimate Human Breeding* (2018), the novella *The Keeper of Chernobyl* (2019), the collections *The Radioactive Bride* (2020), *The Garden of Delight* (2017), *The Monster, the Bad and the Ugly* (2016, with Paolo Di Orazio), and *The Massacre of the Mermaids* (2015), the poetry collections *The Place of Broken Things* (2019, with Linda D. Addison), *War* (2018, with Marge Simon), *No Mercy* (2017), *Sacrificial Nights* (2016, with Bruce Boston) *Eden Underground* (2015), *Venus Intervention* (2014, with Corrine de Winter), and the graphic novel *Calcutta Horror* (2019)

He edited the anthologies *The Beauty of Death* (2016), *The Beauty of Death Vol. 2 - Death by Water* (2017, with Jodi Renee Lester) and *Monsters of Any Kind* (2018, with Daniele Bonfanti)

His stories and poems have appeared in Italian, USA, and UK and Polish magazines, such as Dark Moon Digest, Splatterpunk Zine, Disturbed Digest, Space and Time, Weird Tales Magazine, The Horror Zine, Illumen, Devolution Z, Hinnom, Recompose, Polu Texni, Nothing's Sacred, Okolica Strachu, and anthologies such as *Splatterpunk Forever, Best Hardcore Horror of the Year* Vol. 2, 4 and 5, *The Big Book of Blasphemy, Midnight Under the Big Top, Bones III, Rhysling Anthology* (2015, 2016, 2017, 2018, 2019, 2020), *HWA Poetry Showcase* Vol. 3 and 4, *The Beauty of Death* Vol. 1 and Vol. 2, *Mar Dulce, I Sogni del Diavolo, Danze Eretiche* Vol. 2, *Il Buio Dentro, Sorrow, Pandemonium,*

*Fantatrieste* and many others.

Awards and Nominations:
• Bram Stoker Awards 2019 winner
• Bram Stoker Awards 2015 winner
• SFPA Elgin Awards 2019 winner
• Bram Stoker Awards 2019 three-time nominee
• Bram Stoker Awards 2018 nominee
• Bram Stoker Awards 2017 two-time nominee
• Bram Stoker Awards 2016 two-time nominee
• Bram Stoker Awards 2014 nominee
• Splatterpunk Awards 2019 nominee
• Splatterpunk Awards 2018 nominee
• Rhysling Awards 2015, 2016, 2017, 2018, 2019, 2020 nominee
• Elgin Awards 2015, 2016, 2017, 2018, 2019 nominee
• This is Horror Awards 2017 nominee
• Indie Horror Book Awards 2019 nominee
• HWA Specialty Press Awards 2017 winner (as CEO of Independent Legions Press)

Furthermore, he received honorable mentions (for stories and poems) in Ellen Datlow's '*The Best Horror of the Year*' Vol. 7-8-9-10-12.
He has translated works by Ramsey Campbell, Richard Laymon, Poppy Z. Brite, Edward Lee, Graham Masterton, Gary Braunbeck, Gene O'Neill, Lisa Morton, Lucy Snyder, H. P. Lovecraft, Bram Stoker, Edgar Allan Poe and many others.
He is the CEO & Founder of Independent Legions Publishing, editor of *Molotov Magazine* and *Illégale Magazine* (in Italian), HWA Active member and a former HWA Board of Trustees member.
Website: WWW.BATTIAGO.COM

Alessandro Manzetti
WWW.BATTIAGO.COM

WWW.INDEPENDENTLEGIONS.COM

**NARAKA**
by Alessandro Manzetti
Novel– Paperback and eBook Edition
May 2018


**A WINTER SLEEP**
by Greg F. Gifune
Novel– Paperback and eBook Edition
April 2018


**SPREE AND OTHER STORIES**
by Lucy Taylor
Collection – Paperback and eBook Edition
February 2018


**THE LIVING AND THE DEAD**
by Greg F. Gifune
Novel – Paperback and eBook Edition
December 2017


**TALKING IN THE DARK**
by Dennis Etchison
Collection – eBook Edition
December 2017


**THE BEAUTY OF DEATH 2 – DEATH BY WATER**
edited by Alessandro Manzetti & Jodi Renee Lester
Anthology – Paperback and eBook Edition
November 2017


**DREAMS THE RAGMAN**
by Greg F. Gifune
Novella – Paperback and eBook Edition
November 2017

**CHILDREN OF NO ONE**
by Nicole Cushing
Novella – Paperback and eBook Edition
October 2017


**THE RAIN DANCERS**
by Greg F. Gifune
Novella – Paperback and eBook Edition
September 2017


**THE WISH MECHANICS**
by Daniel Braum
Collection – Paperback and eBook Edition
July 2017


**THE ONE THAT COMES BEFORE**
by Livia Llewellyn
Novella – Paperback and eBook Edition
May 2017


**SELECTED STORIES**
by Nate Southard
Collection – Paperback and eBook Edition
March 2017


**THE CARP-FACED BOY AND OTHER TALES**
by Thersa Matsuura
Collection – Paperback and eBook Edition
February 2017


**DOCTOR BRITE**
by Poppy Z. Brite
Collection – eBook Edition
December 2016


**ALL AMERICAN HORROR OF THE 21ST CENTURY: THE FIRST DECADE**
edited by Mort Castle
Anthology – Paperback and eBook Edition
November 2016

**BENEATH THE NIGHT**
by Greg Gifune
Novel – Paperback and eBook Edition
October 2016

**WHAT WE FOUND IN THE WOODS**
by Shane McKenzie
Collection – eBook Edition
September 2016

**THE HORROR SHOW**
by Poppy Z. Brite
Collection – eBook Edition
August 2016

**THE BEAUTY OF DEATH VOL. 1**
Edited by Alessandro Manzetti
Anthology – eBook Edition
July 2016

**SELECTED STORIES**
by Edward Lee
Collection – eBook Edition
July 2016

**USED STORIES**
by Poppy Z. Brite
Collection – eBook Edition
June 2016

**THE USHERS**
by Edward Lee
Collection – eBook Edition
May 2016

**THE CRYSTAL EMPIRE**
by Poppy Z. Brite
Novella – eBook Edition
April 2016

**SONGS FOR THE LOST**
by Alexander Zelenyj
Collection – eBook Edition
April 2016

**SELECTED STORIES**
by Poppy Z. Brite
Collection – eBook Edition
February 2016

**THE HITCHHIKING EFFECT**
by Gene O'Neill
Collection – eBook Edition
February 2016

WE ARE DARK LEGIONS

WWW.INDEPENDENTLEGIONS.COM

INDEPENDENT LEGIONS PUBLISHING
Via Virgilio, 10 – TRIESTE (ITALY)
+39 040 9776602
www.independentlegions.com
independent.legions@aol.com